Birthday Book
Gray Warden

Making Paper Airplanes

That Really Fly

Making Paper Airplanes

That Really Fly

Nick Robinson

Sterling Publishing Co., Inc.
New York

Creative director: Sarah King
Project editor: Anna Southgate
Designer: 2H Design

Library of Congress Cataloging-in-Publication Data Available

10   9   8   7   6   5   4   3   2   1

Published in 2004 by Sterling Publishing Co.., Inc.
387 Park Avenue South
New York, N.Y. 10016

This book was designed and produced by
D&S Books Ltd
Kerswell, Parkham Ash
Bideford, Devon, EX39 5PR

Distributed in Canada by Sterling Publishing
C/o Canadian Manda Group, 165 Dufferin Street
Toronto, Ontario, Canada M6K 3H6

Manufactured in China

Sterling ISBN: 1-4027-1630-3

1 3 5 7 9 10 8 6 4 2

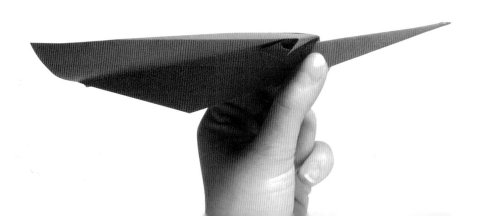

Contents

Introduction

The sight of an airplane passing overhead is commonplace these days, yet people still look upward and watch with fascination as these gleaming machines speed toward their destination. Where does it come from? Where is it going? Who is onboard? We know none of these things, yet the simple fact that they are in the air seems to make their trip mysterious and exotic. For most people, airplanes are a fact of life and have always been there, yet the first flight was just one-hundred years ago. Despite our best efforts, man cannot fly without a machine to help him. However, we can still make other things fly: balloons, gliders, parachutes, and best of all, paper planes.

We don't know when the first paper plane was invented, but the classic "dart" seems to be over a hundred years old. It may have predated the first real plane! As with most paper-folding (often known as origami), the economy of means is a major attraction. You only need paper and your hands, and within thirty seconds or so you can create something that can take to the skies. Since they have no engine, paper planes can glide at best, and won't stay in the air for long. The current world record for time in the air is less than thirty seconds. One of the designs in this book may well beat that record if you are prepared to practice and experiment!

This book aims to take the design of paper planes a small step forward. New techniques for "locking" the sides of the plane together are used, and you are advised to experiment and extend these ideas. One truth about paper-folding is that just when you think that all of the good ideas and designs have been discovered, somebody finds a new one, and you think, "I wish I'd thought of that!" New ideas are waiting in the paper to be discovered with no more than basic folding skills, some imagination, and a bit of dedication.

Making Paper Airplanes

Making a paper plane that flies well is a mixture of science, experimentation, and perseverance. You must be prepared to put some time and effort into it to get the best results. However, it's not beyond anyone to get good results. Here are some of the areas that you should think about when reaching for the stars!

People often expect their planes to fly beautifully the first time round. This is very unlikely to happen! In almost all cases, you need to make adjustments to get the best results from your plane, especially if you want to enter any kind of paper-plane contest. There are three main areas that may need adjustment. The angle of launch, the speed at which you launch, and adjusting (known as "trimming") the wings. Each of them will have a significant effect upon the quality of flight.

Angle of Launch

This refers to the angle that the nose of the plane is pointing at when you let go of it. An angle of zero degrees means launching straightforward. If you do so, the chances are that the plane will start to sink almost immediately. Most paper planes designed for distance need to be launched with a slight upward angle. Others may be better with a steep angle of launch so that they rise quickly into the air before slowly descending again. This is certainly the case when you are competing in a "longest time in the air" competition. The idea here is to get as much height as possible, then have the plane fall into a wide, circular, gliding pattern so that it will take a long time to come down.

Speed of Launching

Paper planes with a large wing area usually need a very gentle launch, since the wing area isn't very strong and will buckle if launched too quickly. More streamlined designs can be launched at a faster pace. Some should be launched as quickly as possible! If you want to compete for "distance" or "time aloft" records, you'll need to develop an aggressive, but controlled, launching action. The aim is to impart as much speed as you can without stressing the paper too much. With every plane you fold, experiment to find out the best launch speed. After a while, you will have some idea before you launch, determined by the plane's characteristics.

Trimming

This means adjusting the wings or any other "sticking-out bits." Probably the most important factor is the angle that the wings form from the center outward. This is known as dihedral. On most designs, you will need a dihedral angle so that the tips of the wings are raised relative to the center of the wings. This will make the plane more stable in flight. The plane may fly better with quite a large angle of dihedral.

How to Create an "A" Proportion Rectangle

Many of the planes in this book are best made from A (letter-size) paper. This is easily made from either a square or any other rectangle, as shown below.

"A" Proportion From a Rectangle

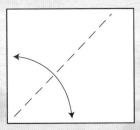

1. Fold one side to an adjacent side, crease, and unfold.

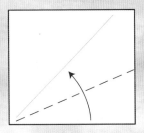

2. Fold the lower edge to the crease.

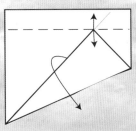

3. Fold the top edge over, making a crease that touches the corner crease, and unfold.

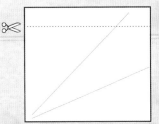

4. Cut along the crease.

"A" Proportion From a Square

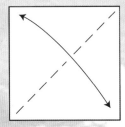

1. Fold one side to an adjacent side, crease, and unfold.

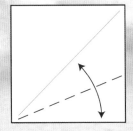

2. Fold the lower edge to the crease.

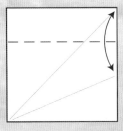

3. Fold the top edge over to meet the end of the crease made in the last step, crease, and unfold.

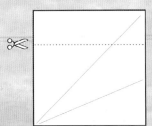

4. Cut along the crease.

Another key adjustment area is the back of the wings, or "trailing edges." If the plane tends to dive too steeply and seems heavy at the nose end, add a very slight upward curl to the back of the wings. Be sure to make any adjustments small ones, giving the plane a test launch after each one. You will soon learn the right amount of "tweak" to apply to the wing.

To confuse matters, these three factors will affect each other. Launching more slowly, you may need a greater dihedral. Curling the wingtips, you may need a steeper angle of launch. The only way to find out is to make a single change, then fly the plane and watch how it performs. Keep adjusting until you have fine-tuned the plane. After a while, you will learn to do this quickly, and will know how to cure various flight problems.

Conditions
Paper planes are usually very lightweight, and so are easily affected by wind. The only sensible answer to this problem is to fly your planes inside and keep all windows and doors shut. Good locations include gymnasiums, halls, large garages, and so on. An ideal location has no wind or drafts, a length of 300 feet, and a height of 100 feet. The only place in which you can find this is in sports arenas or aircraft hangars, which can prove expensive to hire, but it is worth it. You can then break some world records!

Paper has a tendency to absorb moisture from the air. This means that your plane's wings will start to sag after a while. There is no cure for this (other than a warm, dry room), so you should be prepared to "retire" your plane after a fairly limited lifespan. You should then fold another! The frustrating part is that no matter how carefully you fold two apparently identical planes, one may be a great flier, the other hopeless. This is part of the fun: if it were easy to predict flight characteristics, the whole process would become mechanical. The reality of the situation is that a raw beginner can strike lucky and get very impressive results.

Optional Extras
Many paper-plane enthusiasts are quite strict when making paper planes: they will only use folding techniques to achieve their results. Others use adhesive tape, weights, cuts, extra pieces, anything it takes to help the plane fly. The rules for the paper-plane world record (both for distance and for time in the air) allow you to use small pieces of tape to keep the wings together.

A few years ago, following a suggestion from the British Origami Society, a new category was added, which insists on the use of pure origami techniques, with no cuts or use of tape. This has encouraged many paper-folders to have a go at designing paper planes: some of the exciting designs are featured within this book. Many children like to tear small flaps in the wings to make them look better and possibly improve the flight. The use of flaps can certainly allow you to make fine adjustments to the "trim" of the plane, but you may feel that it is less satisfactory than "pure" folding.

Tips for Folding From This Book

Make sure that your hands are clean before folding!

Fold on a flat surface, such as a table.

Don't rush the model: fold slowly, carefully, and neatly.

If you don't quite understand the photos, read the words as well.

Make each plane three times. The last should fly much more effectively than the first!

Be creative: alter angles and distances to see if you can improve the flight pattern.

Everyone has his or her own standards, and you should do whatever makes you happy! It is also true that adding some weight to the front end of a plane (in the form of a paper clip) will often make it fly better, but you may think that is cheating.

Choosing Paper

The choice of paper patterns is entirely up to you, but be warned that some types of paper (for example, sugar paper) do not make very good planes if they are not crisp enough. Some types of paper will absorb moisture from the air more quickly and should be avoided. If the design is very complicated, you may need thinner paper, as above a certain size, the plane simply won't fly at all.

Standard American A (letter-size) or European A4 paper is perfect for most uses and is cheap to buy. Tracing paper is light, but strong, making it great for planes. See page 10 for how to create A- (letter-size-) proportioned paper from a different-shaped rectangle or a square.

Creating Your Own Designs

When you fold the more complicated paper planes, you may be in awe of the people who created them. They may seem talented and artistic, but this isn't always the case. Many simply adapt ideas from other designs and add a few new touches. If you start with a simple design, you can alter distances, change some of the angles, add extra creases, and miss some creases. Eventually, you'll have an original design!

When testing your designs, carry out test flights after each change to see what effect it had. If it flies properly, you have adapted it successfully. If not, start with a new sheet and try some different changes. Don't keep altering the same model because the paper will have unwanted creases. Since paper is so cheap, it will cost very little! If you know someone who works in an office, they probably throw away hundreds of sheets of paper every week. A polite request should get you as much folding material as you need.

There is no simple route to being creative, but you must have patience and be prepared to break any rules that get in your way. For example, most planes start by us folding the long edges of the paper together. Why not try the opposite: fold the short edges together instead? Designs such as the "landscape" and "Alison" started this way. You may find problems that will need ingenuity and patience to solve, but your designs are more likely to be original. Something else you may like to try is the "Holy Grail" of paper planes: asymmetrical designs. These are shapes that are not symmetrical; the wings may be a different shape. Many say that it is impossible to create such a plane, but who knows?

Competitions

If you are serious about paper planes, you'll want to challenge some of the world records by entering or setting up competitions. There are a number of categories for which there are international records. These include "time aloft" (how long you can keep your plane in the air (which is currently over twenty seconds) and "distance," how far you can make a paper plane travel (the current record stands at nearly 200 feet). Many professional competitors use small lengths of adhesive tape to keep the sides of the plane together. However, there is now an official category for "origami," where the design must only use folding techniques. World-record-holders take their hobby very seriously and put in hours of practice, building up the specific muscles that are used to launch a plane. If you want to hold a competition at work or school, all you really need is a large, open space with no wind. To attempt a world record, you'll need a large aircraft hangar! You can also organize less serious categories, such as acrobatics, most decorative design, worst flyer(!), and most entertaining launch technique.

Societies

Around the world, you'll find small groups of people who are devoted to paper planes. You may have more success by joining origami societies. There is at least one in every major country in the world. You will be able read a regular magazine, buy proper paper, and get your hands on books featuring paper planes. Perhaps most importantly, you'll make contact with lots of other people who enjoy paper-folding. People who do origami (the Japanese word for paper-folding) are usually very friendly, and will help you with any folding problems you may have. Many origamists are keen paper-plane flyers in their spare time. Here are two of the largest web-sites.

British Origami Society www.britishorigami.org.uk

Origami U.S.A. www.ousa.com

At the Time of Writing, the Current Records Are:

TIME ALOFT

Guinness World Record   **27.6** seconds, set by *Ken Blackburn,* 1998.

Guinness British Record   **20.9** seconds, set by *Chris Edge & Andy Currey,* July 28, 1996.

Origami Record   **20.9** seconds, set by *Andy Currey,* July 28, 1996.

DISTANCE

Guinness World Record   **193** feet (58.8m), set by *Tony Fletch,* May 21, 1985.

Guinness British Record   **104** feet (31.7m), set by *Andy Currey,* September 19, 1997.

Origami Record   **94** feet (28.7m), set by *Robin Glynne,* September 19, 1997.

Glossary of Aviation Terms

Aileron: a moveable part of an airplane's wing, which makes an airplane roll.

Airfoil: the wing of an airplane, which produces lift.

Angle of attack: the angle at which the wings meet the air.

Asymmetrical: a design with wings that are a different shape to each other.

Barnstormer: a plane designed to perform aerobatics.

Canard: a design where the tail is at the front rather than the rear.

Center of gravity: the point at which a plane balances.

Control surfaces: moveable parts of the plane that control flight.

Elevator: a part of the tail that tilts an airplane up or down.

Flight pattern: the path that a plane makes through the air.

Fuselage: the main body of the plane.

Laminar-flow wing: a wing that creates less air resistance (drag) than a normal wing.

Leading edges: the front edges of a wing.

Lift: a force that acts on the wings to move the plane upward.

Mach number: mach 1 is the speed of sound.

Pitch: when the tail of the plane moves up or down.

Trailing edges: the back edges of the wing.

Ornithopter: an old-fashioned type of flying machine that looks like a bird.

Rudder: the vertical part of a tail.

Roll: when one wing moves up as the other moves down.

Rate of roll: the speed at which the airplane rolls.

Stable: when a plane flies straight and level without rolling, pitching, or yawing.

Stall: when the plane loses control and drops from the sky!

Supersonic: an airplane capable of exceeding the speed of sound.

Swept-wing: a design where leading and trailing edges of a wing point backward.

Unstable: when a plane changes direction without control.

V.T.O.L.: vertical take-off and landing, an aircraft that can fly straight upward.

Yaw: when one wing moves forward as the other moves backward.

Wingtip: the outer end of an airplane's wing.

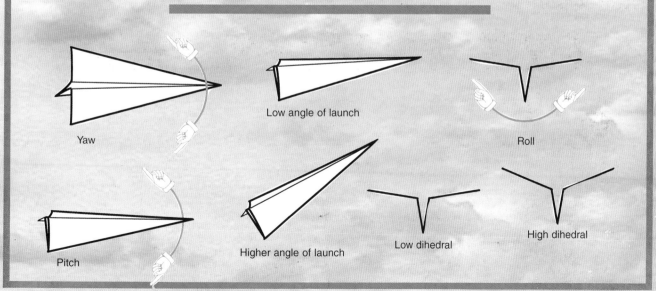

Yaw

Low angle of launch

Roll

Pitch

Higher angle of launch

Low dihedral

High dihedral

The Projects

The projects in this book should ideally be folded in order, since some of the later designs may present less detailed explanation of moves and techniques that are covered in earlier designs. More experienced folders may pick and choose. Remember to fold slowly and carefully, checking ahead to see what you are aiming for with each step. Make your first few models using any paper that you can lay your hands on. Once you've mastered the sequence, you may want to use slightly better-quality paper.

Turnover symbol

Classic Dart

There can be few people who have never enjoyed the pleasure of launching this simple design. No one knows exactly how old it is, but it may even predate the first "real" airplane! It's a good opportunity to practice making neat, accurate creases. As with all paper models, if you take your time, the result will look much more impressive.

2. Fold the lower left-hand corner in so that the short edge lies along the central crease. The completed fold is shown on the other side.

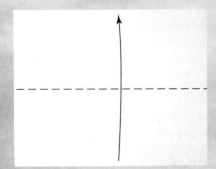

1. Fold one long side to meet the other; adjust until they are perfectly lined up. Hold the layers in position with one hand, then crease firmly, and unfold.

3. Make a similar fold by taking the folded edge to meet the central crease. The completed fold is shown on the other side. Remember to make sharp creases.

4. Fold the plane in half along the central crease to produce this step.

5. Fold the wingtip to meet the original halfway crease. Turn the paper round so that you can fold away from yourself, as this makes life easier.

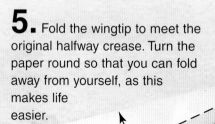

6. This is the result. Repeat the fold with the other wing.

7. Because this design has a sharp point at one end, it may be dangerous to fly it toward people. To make it safer, it's a good idea to cut or tear the sharp point off. You'll be surprised to see that this produces a miniplane!

FLIGHT ADVICE

Launch
Medium-strength at a slight upward angle.

Trim
The wings should have a slight upward angle (dihedral).

Creative Suggestions
Try turning the paper over before step 3. Try folding in half using a mountain crease in step 4.

8. Complete!

Classic Glider

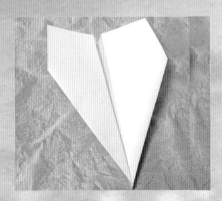

This is another tried-and-tested design. The idea of "locking" the flaps together using the triangular tab was first suggested by a Japanese paper-plane expert called Eiji Nakamura. When trimmed properly, it is a superb glider, yet it is simple and quick to make.

1. Fold one long side to meet the other, crease firmly, and unfold.

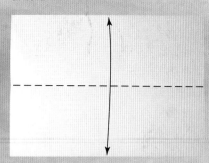

2. Fold both halves of a short edge to lie along the central crease, as with the classic dart. Leave a small "fudge factor" (see the next step).

3. Because paper planes can often be several layers thick, folding in half toward the final stages can be awkward. To help, we often leave a small gap when folding in to the central crease. American folders refer to this as a "fudge factor."

4. Fold the end of the triangle to the right, almost to the end of the central crease, leaving a gap about as wide as your thumb (it isn't critical). Refer to the next picture for guidance.

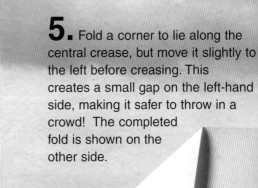

5. Fold a corner to lie along the central crease, but move it slightly to the left before creasing. This creates a small gap on the left-hand side, making it safer to throw in a crowd! The completed fold is shown on the other side.

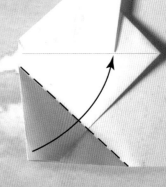

6. Swing the small triangle to the left, overlapping the two corners. This "locks" them in place during flight.

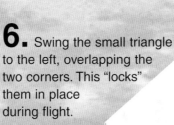

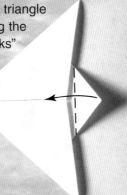

7. Mountain-fold the plane in half, swinging the lower half underneath.

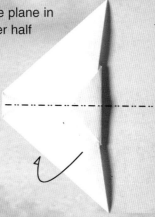

8. This is the result. Turn the paper around.

9. Starting at the corner of the blunted nose, fold the wings past the lower edge. Refer to the next picture for guidance.

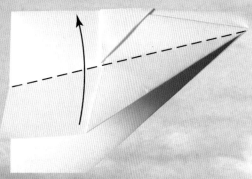

10. This is the result. The hidden edge is shown in X-ray view. Repeat with the other wing.

11. Complete.

FLIGHT ADVICE

Launch
Medium-strength at a slight upward angle.

Trim
The wings should have slight upward angle (dihedral).

Creative Suggestions
Alter the fold used to create the wings in step 10, making the wings firstly bigger, then smaller. How does this affect the flight? If you don't "lock" the flaps, does it make a difference?

Hawk

This is another design with a long history, having been around since at least the 1930s. It uses an elegant series of origami techniques to create the nose section. You should make this design several times until you are confident with the folding method. Start with the central crease in place.

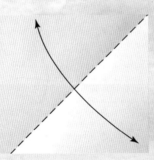

1. Fold a short edge over to meet a long edge. Crease firmly and unfold.

2. Repeat the fold to the other long edge (the picture shows this step before it is unfolded).

3. Open the paper out. Turn the paper over so that the creases that you have made are now mountain folds.

MAKING PAPER AIRPLANES

6. This is the result. The triangular section is known as a "waterbomb base" in the origami world.

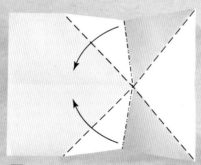

4. Fold the corners to meet the ends of the diagonal creases. Crease and unfold.

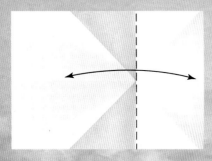

5. Turn the paper over and use the creases to collapse the paper into a triangular shape.

7. Fold one of the loose corners to the tip of the triangle.

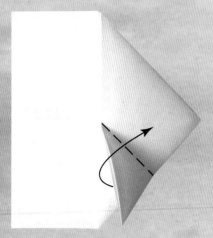

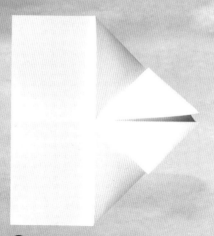

8. Repeat on the other corner. This is the result.

9. Turn the paper around to this position. Fold the two loose corners to the opposite corner of the internal square, taking the layer underneath with them. Crease carefully (due to the thickness) and unfold.

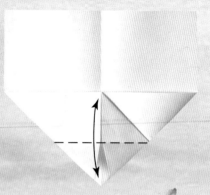

11. Repeat the last step with the lower right-hand side of the square. Repeat the last two steps on the upper side of the square.

10. Turn the paper back to the previous position. Fold one side of the square to meet the horizontal crease. Crease and unfold.

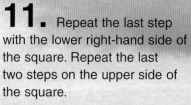

12. Fold in two upper sides of the square, pressing the center together into a point. Repeat on the other side.

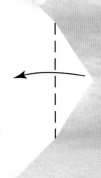

13. Turn the paper over and fold in the tip on an existing crease. The crease is a mountain, which you'll need to change to a valley. Fold carefully and enjoy the way that the folds move into position.

14. Now valley-fold in half along the central crease.

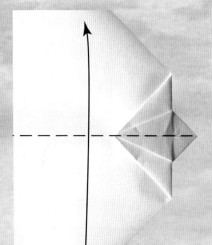

15. This is the result.

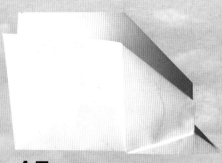

16. Fold down one of the wings, parallel to the lower edge, starting at the top of the nose section.

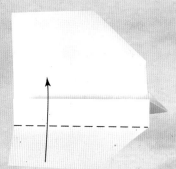

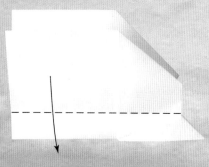

17. Then fold it back up, level with the base of the plane.

18. Fold it back down once more and repeat with the other wing. You can experiment with the position of these pleats.

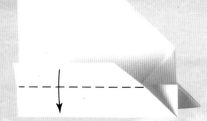

19. Complete.

Test Plane

By *Nick Robinson.*
This design will help you explore the effect that
various wing configurations can have upon the flight pattern.
You can use these ideas when exploring variations of
the other designs in this book.

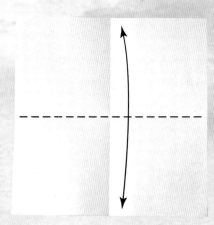

1. Start with a square creased in half. Fold in half, crease, and unfold.

2. Fold two corners to the center, crease, and unfold.

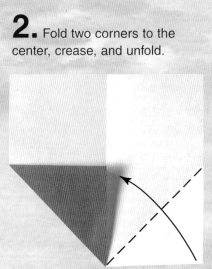

3. Fold in two edges to meet the creases made in the last step. Swing both flaps over on existing creases.

MAKING PAPER AIRPLANES

5. Rotate the paper. Follow the creases shown to form a central point, which you swing downward.

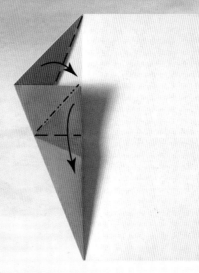

4. Fold over one side along the inside edge. Repeat with the other flap, leaving it in place.

6. Pull out the layer of paper from within the layers.

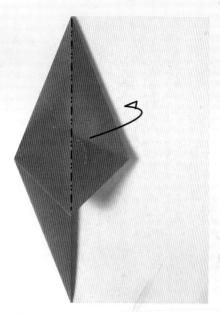

8. Fold over the whole colored section on an existing crease.

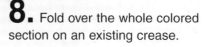

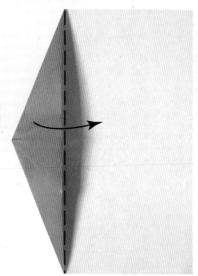

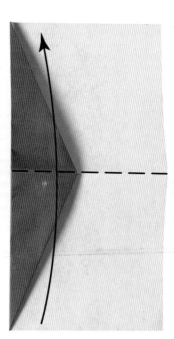

7. Tuck the layer underneath.

9. Fold the paper in half.

10. Fold down both wings to form a narrow body.

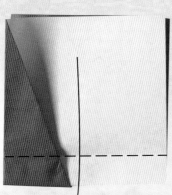

12. Here, two wingtips have been folded up. Try folding them down for comparison.

11. This is the basic shape, to which you can add variations.

13. Further creases make a more complicated profile.

14. You can go as far as you like, but try each step to see if it helps the flight, or hinders it.

FLIGHT ADVICE

Launch
Experiment!

Trim
Experiment!

Creative Suggestions
Experiment!

How to Hold Your Plane

Canard

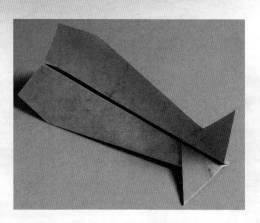

Traditional, arranged by **Nick Robinson.**
This is a well-known variation on the traditional dart, where the original corners are allowed to point outward instead of being folded away. The term *canard* (which is French for "duck") refers to aircraft with some kind of stabilizers at the front end.

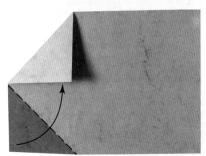

1. Start with an A (letter-size) piece of paper or similar rectangle, creased in half. Fold two corners to the center.

2. Turn the paper over and take the folded edges to the center, allowing the corners to pop out again. Unfold these flaps.

3. Fold the lower left-hand edge to the crease you made in the last step. (This step is not used in the traditional design.)

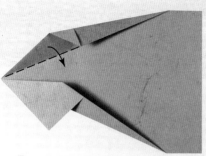

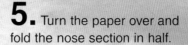

5. Turn the paper over and fold the nose section in half.

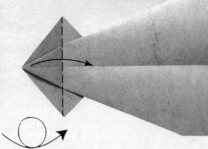

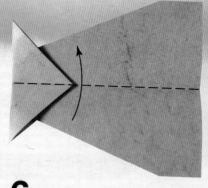

4. Refold the flaps on the existing creases.

6. This is the result; fold in half.

7. Fold down both wings to the long, folded edge.

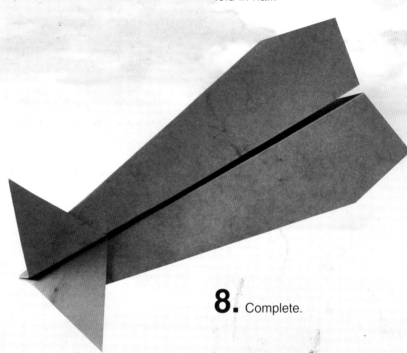

8. Complete.

How to Hold Your Plane

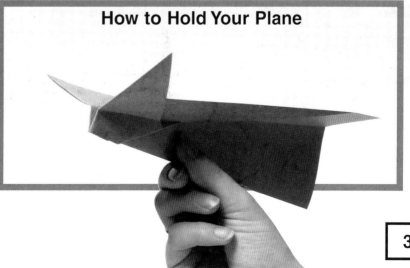

Championship

Traditional.
This is the basic design used by many of the current
record-breakers in the paper-airplane world, to which they add a
strip of adhesive tape to keep the wings together. As you will see,
it flies beautifully without the tape.

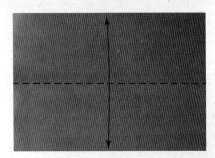

1. Start with an A (letter-size)
rectangle. Fold one long side to
meet the other, crease firmly,
and unfold.

2. Fold the left-hand corners
to lie along the central crease.
Don't forget to include a small
fudge factor.

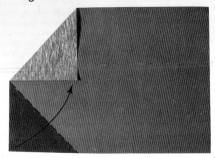

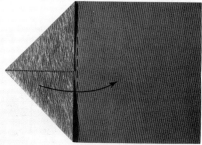

3. Fold over the triangular
shape along the inside edge.

4. Fold in two corners as in step 2, then unfold both sides.

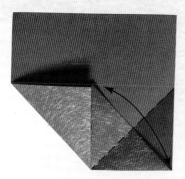

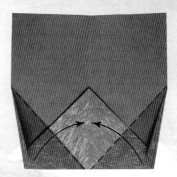

5. Mountain-fold the plane in half. Fold over the corner at a slight angle, starting at the end of the crease. Turn over and match up the other side.

6. Open up the folds back to the start of step 4. With the small creases in place, refold the existing creases.

7. This is the result. Fold over the small triangular flap to "lock" the loose flaps, then mountain-fold the plane in half.

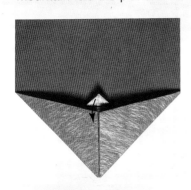

8. Mountain-fold the plane in half again. Fold down the wings: the crease starts at the tip of the nose and passes through the top of the tiny triangle.

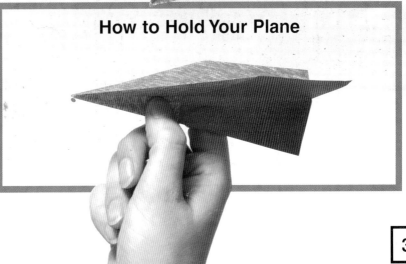

9. Complete.

FLIGHT ADVICE

Launch
Launch with a firm forward release; try different angles of release.

Trim
As ever, adjust the wing angles.

Creative Suggestions
Alter the angle at which the wings are folded down in step 8.

How to Hold Your Plane

Hoop

By **Nick Robinson.**

There are very few circular designs that fly. This one is a variation on a similar traditional design made from a square of paper.

1. Start with a sheet of A-size paper or a similar rectangle. Fold the bottom left-hand corner to meet the top right-hand corner.

2. Fold in half along the folded edge . . .

3. . . . like this. Crease firmly and unfold completely.

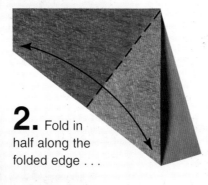

4. You have now created a crease that runs from corner to opposite corner. Fold along that crease.

5. Make a pinch mark to locate the halfway point of the central crease.

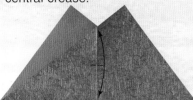

6. Take the folded edge to meet the pinch mark.

7. Carefully fold the outside edge to the inside edge. Crease and unfold.

8. Form the paper into a tube and start to feed one end into the other.

9. Finally, refold the crease made in step 7 to lock the paper together. Make sure that you hold the interlocking flaps together as you start.

10. Once in place, run your fingers around the edge to make it smooth and circular.

11. Complete.

FLIGHT ADVICE

Launch
The thin part of the loop should be on top. Hold it by the sides or the lower rear end and push it forward at a medium speed.

Creative Suggestions
Alter the amount folded in during steps 6 and 7. Try to make the same design starting with a square.

How to Hold Your Plane

Radford

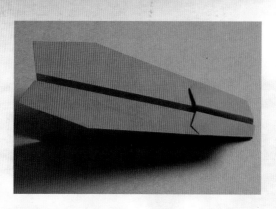

By **Nick Robinson.**
This attractive sequence of folds creates a glider that performs
very well. It was named in memory of Mark Radford,
an origami-enthusiast friend of the author.

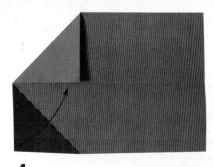

1. Start with a sheet of A-sized paper, creased in half. Fold in a corner to lie along the central crease. Repeat with the matching corner.

2. Fold in the tip to meet the two corners.

3. Swing the thicker section back over, along the inside raw edges.

5. Fold the outer edges of the wings to lie along the central crease. Crease and unfold.

4. Turn the paper over. If you flatten the paper, you'll be able to see the hidden edge underneath. Fold the tips of the thicker section to touch the central crease at this point.

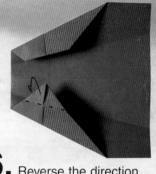

6. Reverse the direction of the creases to fold the small sections underneath.

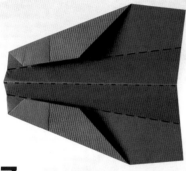

7. Form the classic paper-plane profile using existing creases.

8. Complete.

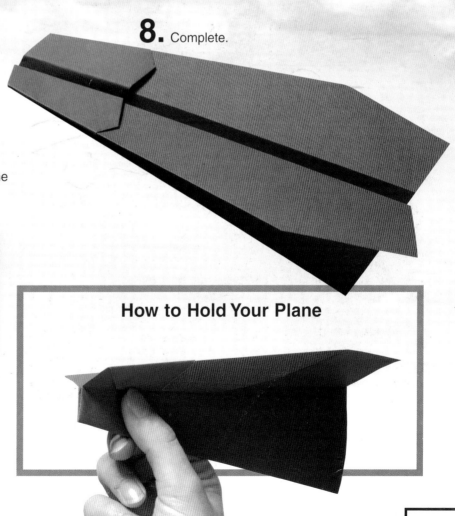

How to Hold Your Plane

FLIGHT ADVICE

Launch
Medium-strength at a slight upward angle.

Trim
The wings should have a slight upward angle (dihedral).

Creative Suggestions
Alter the distances in steps 2 and 3.

Flying Square

By **Nick Robinson**.

This design is unusual in that it starts with a square and finishes with a square! The design arranges internal layers of paper toward the front, so that the center of gravity will allow for a gliding flight.

1. Start with a square, white side facing upward. Fold in half from corner to corner, crease, and unfold.

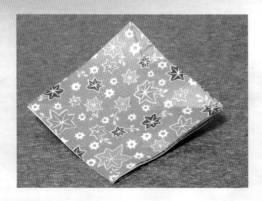

2. Turn the paper around by 90 degrees and fold in half from corner to corner again. The picture shows the finished step.

3. Fold the left-hand corner to the top corner. The completed fold is shown on the right.

4. Fold the right-hand triangle in half toward you. The completed fold is shown on the left.

5. Fold the upper edge of the right-hand triangular section to meet the outside edge. The completed fold is shown on the other side.

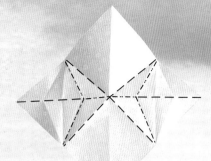

6. Open out the paper completely and turn over to the white side. Alter the creases shown to match the direction indicated.

7. Start to form the paper into a 3D shape, bringing the farthest corner toward you. The paper will collapse into a small square. Refer to the next picture for guidance.

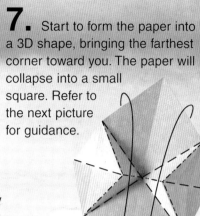

8. This should be the result. If not, unfold and check that you have used the correct mountain and valley creases. Use existing creases to fold the small flaps into a pocket.

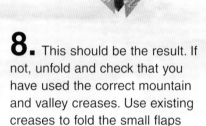

10. Curl the edges upward to complete.

9. One flap is in place, the other is being tucked in.

FLIGHT ADVICE

Launch
Hold by the rear corner, above your head, and launch with a gentle forward release. Try it from a high building!

Trim
The outer wingtips should be curled upward.

How to Hold Your Plane

Sallas

By **Nick Robinson.**

This design is named after a talented German creator called Joan Sallas. It starts with a smaller sheet of paper than the usual A (letter size). You can also try many of the other designs in this book with smaller paper to see how they perform.

1. Start with a sheet of paper measuring 5 x 8 inches, creased in half. Fold the short edges together, pinching the center point.

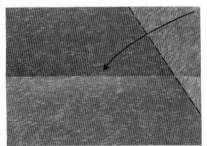

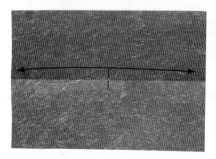

2. Fold a corner to lie exactly on the center point.

3. Repeat with the other corner.

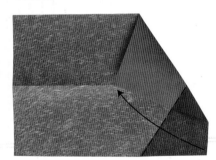

5. Turn the paper over, then fold each half of the short edge to the central crease.

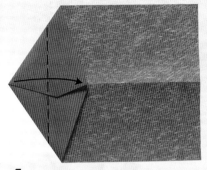

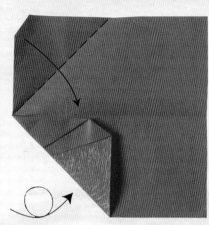

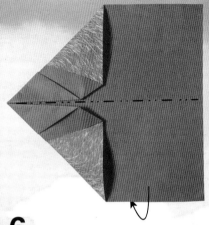

4. Now fold in the tip to the same place.

6. Fold the plane in half.

7. Fold over the wing along the crease shown.

8. Complete.

FLIGHT ADVICE

Launch
Moderate speed, straight forward.

Trim
Keep the wings almost horizontal.

Creative Suggestions
Alter the angles of the wings.

How to Hold Your Plane

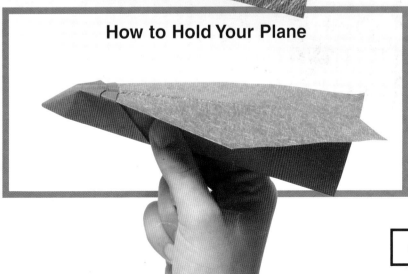

Triplane

By **Nick Robinson.**

Unlike most paper planes, this design uses a 60-degree geometry. It is quite easy to create this angle, and there are many exciting designs waiting to be discovered using these techniques.

1. Start with a square, folded in half. Fold in both sides to the central crease.

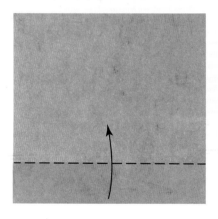

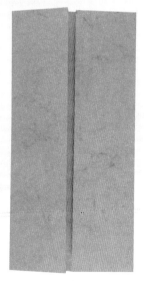

2. This is the result. Turn the paper over.

3. Fold one edge to the central crease and make a gentle crease about one-third the length of the paper.

4. Make a crease that starts in the middle of the short edge. The corner that you fold in should just touch the crease that you made in the last step.

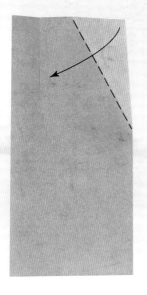

5. Rotate the paper and fold the other corner to lie along the crease made in the last step.

6. Open out the paper fully: you can see the 60-degree triangles formed. Fold in, making your crease pass through the inside corners of the triangles.

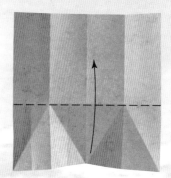

7. Using existing creases, fold in one corner, flattening the outside point.

8. Repeat the move with the other corner.

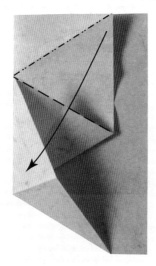

9. Pull out a layer of paper to tuck the point within a pocket underneath.

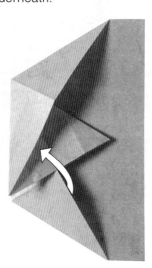

MAKING PAPER AIRPLANES

11. Take the folded front edge of the wing to lie along the center. Repeat with the other wing.

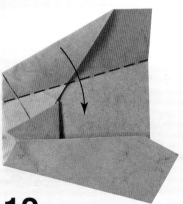

10. Fold the point over.

12. Form the classic plane profile to complete the design.

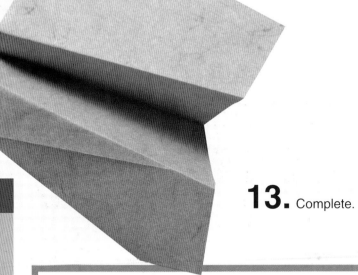

13. Complete.

FLIGHT ADVICE

Launch
Moderate to fast speed, in any direction.

Trim
Adjust the wing angles.

Creative Suggestions
Start at step 6 and design a new plane of your own!

How to Hold Your Plane

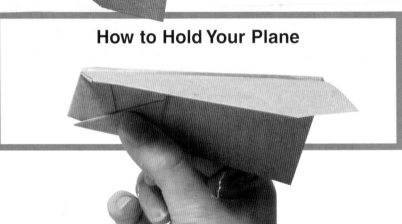

The Alison

By **Nick Robinson.**
This is a slow, stable glider that doesn't use the familiar "short sides to the center" technique of many planes. Instead, the paper is folded in half, then half of the paper is tucked back into the nose section to generate the proper center of gravity.

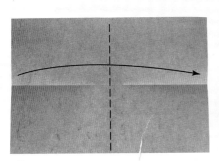

1. Crease a sheet of A-size paper or rectangle in half, between the long edges. Fold the two short edges together.

2. Fold the raw edges to the central crease.

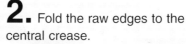

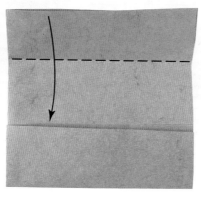

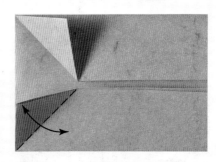

3. Fold the short edges of the left-hand layers back to the long edges, crease, and unfold.

MAKING PAPER AIRPLANES

4. Swing open the first of the layers, pressing the top corner into a triangle using existing creases.

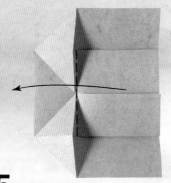

5. Swing the central section to the left.

6. Fold the lower edge to touch the upper edge of the section that you have just folded. Repeat for the other side.

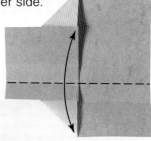

7. Turn the paper over and fold the smaller flap over the folded edge, crease, and unfold back to step 5.

8. Using the creases that you added in steps 5 and 7, tuck the central flap into the pocket.

9. Refold the central crease through the nose section and adjust the profile to that shown in the final image.

FLIGHT ADVICE

Launch
Hold the plane gently at the center. Launch with a gentle forward push.

Trim
Adjust the various angles of the wings.

Creative Suggestions
Can you find an imaginative way of using the "spare" paper in step 8?

How to Hold Your Plane

Stump

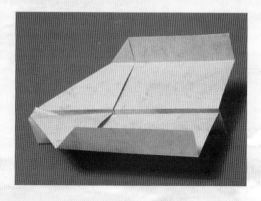

By **Nick Robinson.**

This is another example of how a traditional design can be worked upon to incorporate new ideas. Here, some of the surplus paper at the nose end is overlapped to lock the nose section together and make the design more stable in flight.

1. Crease a sheet of A-size paper or similar rectangle in half. Fold one short edge over to both sides, as in the hawk.

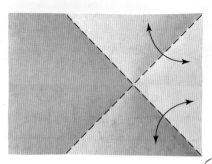

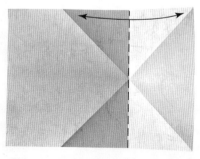

2. Turn the paper over and fold the short edge to the end of the creases.

3. Turn it back over again and use the creases to collapse the paper into the familiar triangular form.

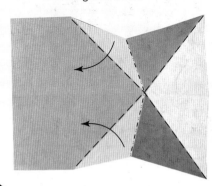

MAKING PAPER AIRPLANES

4. Fold the tips of the triangles into the center.

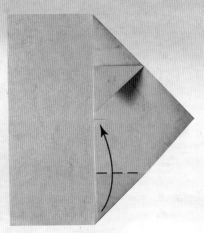

5. Fold the outer corners into the center.

6. Fold the outer corner of the square section into the center and make a horizontal crease the full length of the plane. There are many layers, so fold carefully. Repeat on the other side.

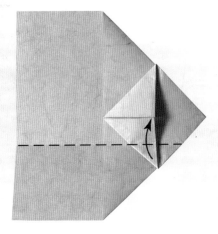

7. Fold the nose into the center of the square section.

8. Fold the lower left-hand edge of the central square to the center. Repeat on the other side, but leave a large fudge factor to allow for the thickness of the paper.

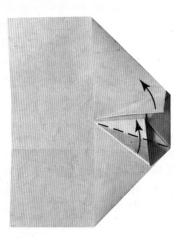

9. Fold the body in half and tuck one flap over the other to lock the body together.

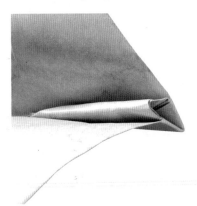

10. Fold down the wings.

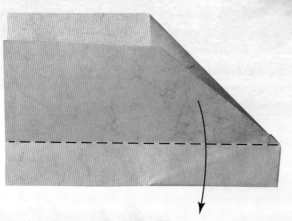

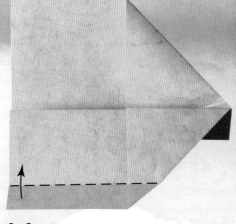

11. Then fold the wingtips back up.

12. Complete!

FLIGHT ADVICE

Launch
Gentle to moderate speed, directly forward.

Trim
Adjust the wing angles.

Creative Suggestions
Try making radical changes to the wing profile.

How to Hold Your Plane

Star Fighter

By **Nick Robinson.**

This design makes use of the two layers of paper created in the first step to create double-sided wingtips. There are very few designs that create this type of wing profile—why not try to create one of your own?

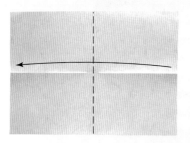

1. Crease a sheet of A-size paper or a rectangle in half. Fold the two short edges together.

2. Take each half of the folded edge to the center, crease firmly, and unfold.

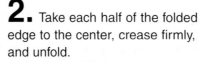

3. Fold the edge to the crease made in the last step, then unfold again.

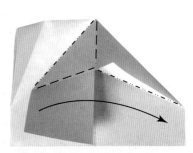

4. Alter the creases as necessary, making the longest one a mountain and the shorter one a valley, on both layers of paper. If you then reform the creases, the paper will collapse into the position shown. Look at the picture closely!

50

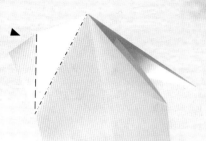

5. Repeat on the other wing.

6. Fold the model in half.

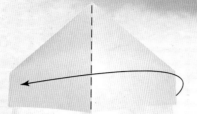

7. Make a crease to form the body (the exact position isn't critical). You can also do this by folding each wing separately.

8. Fold the tip of the nose to the point where the hidden layers meet inside.

9. Swing the flap over once more.

10. Use the edges of the nose section as a reference to fold the sides of the wings to. You should repeat this on the three other flaps.

11. Open out into the profile shown.

FLIGHT ADVICE

Launch
Launch at speed, at most angles.

Trim
Keep the wings at right angles to the body; adjust the wingtips symmetrically.

Creative Suggestions
Try alternative wing profiles.

How to Hold Your Plane

Landscape

By **_Nick Robinson._**
This plane is so called because, unlike most paper airplanes,
it uses a sheet of paper that is in the landscape format (wider
than it is high). Most designs start with the paper in portrait format.
If you want to create truly original designs,
this layout is more likely to give you results!

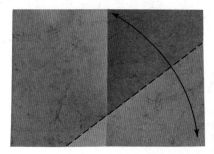

1. Crease an A-size sheet or similar rectangle in half between the short edges. Take the bottom right-hand corner to the top center, crease, and unfold.

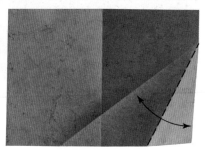

2. Fold the outside edge to the crease that you have just made, crease, and unfold.

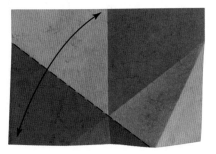

3. Repeat step 1 on the left-hand side.

4. Make a valley=fold from the bottom left-hand corner to the end of the crease on the top.

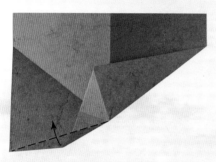

5. Now make a fold similar to that made in step 2 on the left-hand side.

6. Using the existing creases, swing the paper over and tuck it underneath the layers on the right.

7. Mountain-fold the paper in half.

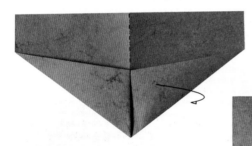

9. Fold back the wing at a slight angle so that the corner of the wingtip is behind the rear edge of the plane.

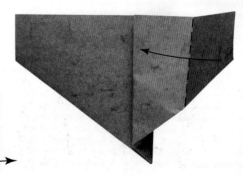

8. Fold most of the wing away from you (the exact distance isn't critical).

53

10. Fold back the tip again so that the rear edge of this tip is vertical.

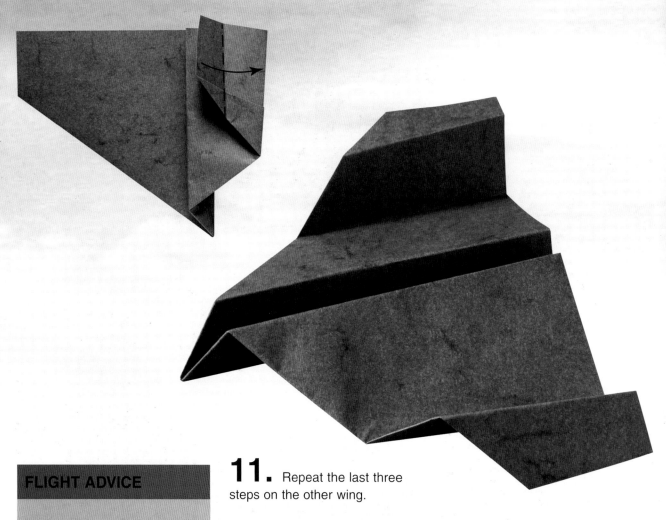

11. Repeat the last three steps on the other wing.

FLIGHT ADVICE

Launch
Open the wings to match the final photograph. Launch with medium strength at a slight upward angle.

Trim
The end section of the wings should be at the same angle as the largest wing section.

Creative Suggestions
Starting at step 8, create your own design!

How to Hold Your Plane

Lock Glider

By *Nick Robinson.*
The body (or fuselage) of most paper airplanes tends to open during flight. However, using some origami ingenuity, it is possible to lock the nose together to prevent this from happening.

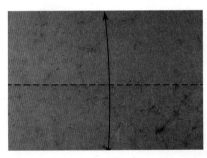

2. Fold the two left-hand corners into the center crease. Leave a slight fudge factor.

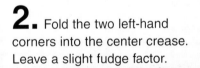

1. Start with a sheet of A-size paper or similar rectangle. Fold the two long sides together, crease, and unfold.

3. Now fold in the wings once more, as in the traditional dart. Unfold again.

4. Fold part of the raw edge to lie along the crease made in the last step.

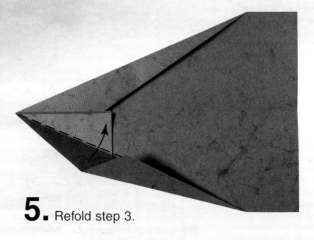

5. Refold step 3.

6. Fold the edges of the nose section to lie along the center crease, but only crease from the tail section as far as the folded edges.

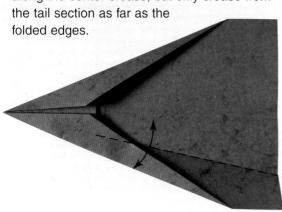

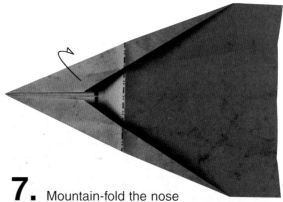

7. Mountain-fold the nose behind. The fold passes through the point where the creases made in the last step meet the folded edges.

8. Turn the paper over. Fold back the sharp tip to the inside of the triangular section.

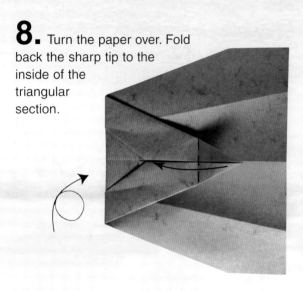

9. Valley-fold the whole plane in half.

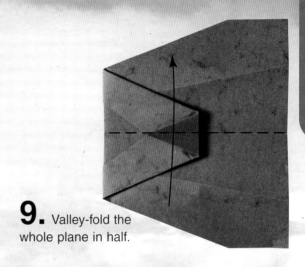

10. Fold over the tip of the nose along an inside edge (you should be able both to see and feel this edge). Crease and unfold.

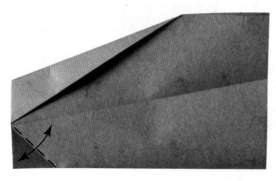

11. Open the top of the plane and push the triangular flap inside, using the crease that you made in the last step. Lift up the left-hand flap and tuck the paper underneath.

12. In progress . . .

13. . . . the step complete. You should be able to refold the plane in half again, with the nose section locked.

14. Complete.

FLIGHT ADVICE

Launch
Medium-strength, at a slight upward angle.

Trim
Alter the angle of the wings to the body. Make sure that the rear corners of the wings are not curled up or down.

Creative Suggestions
In step 6, make a fold at right angles to the tail to create a thin, equal body shape. Continue as before. This variation should be a slow glider.

How to Hold Your Plane

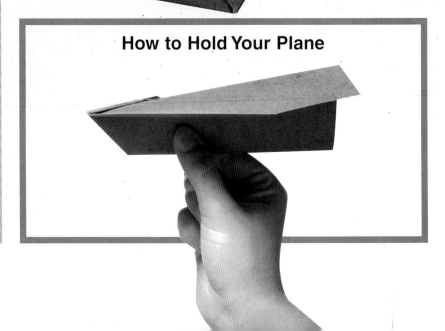

Needle Dart

By **Nick Robinson.**

This is an ultramodern design, sleek and stylish. It uses the "squash" technique taken from traditional origami.

1. Crease a sheet of A-size paper or rectangle in half. Fold two corners to the center.

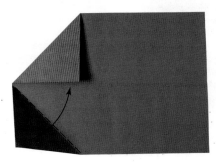

2. Take the folded edges to the center as well.

3. Turn the paper over and fold the edges of the sharp end to the center. These creases only need to extend about one-third of the length.

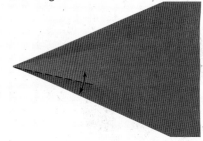

59

MAKING PAPER AIRPLANES

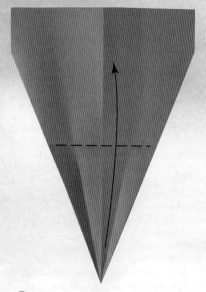

4. Fold the tip to the center of the opposite end.

5. Fold the same point back along the hidden inside edges formed in step 1.

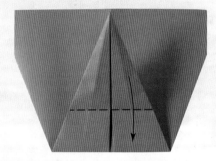

6. Fold the edges of the pointed flap into the center, carefully squashing the paper at the end. See the next picture for guidance. Repeat with the other side.

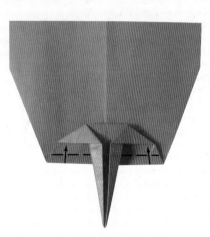

7. Fold the short edge underneath the point in half.

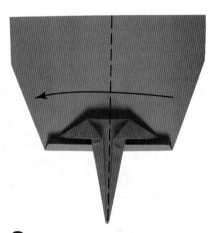

8. Fold in half along the center.

9. Fold the wings down on the line formed by the top of the pointed nose. Crease and unfold.

11. Push the tail inside the body so that it sticks out the other side.

10. Precrease a tail flap.

12. Complete.

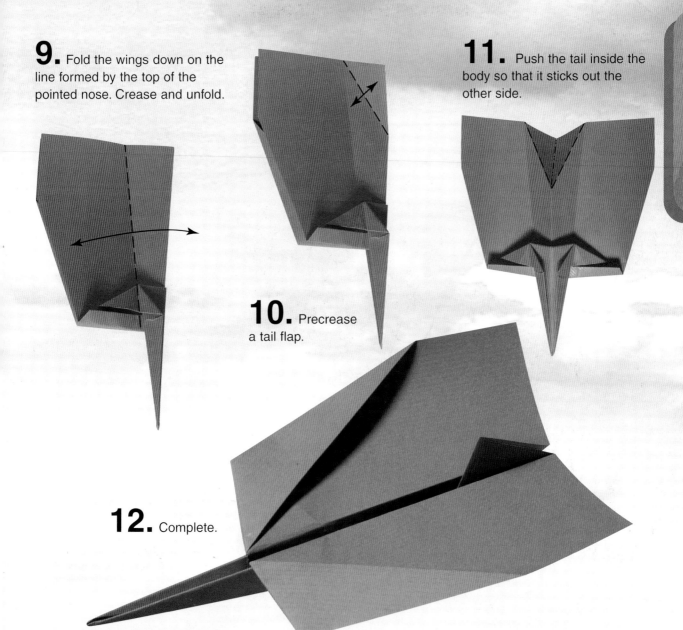

FLIGHT ADVICE

Launch
A steady speed, slightly upward.

Trim
As ever, the wings.

Creative Suggestions
Try alternative wing profiles.

How to Hold Your Plane

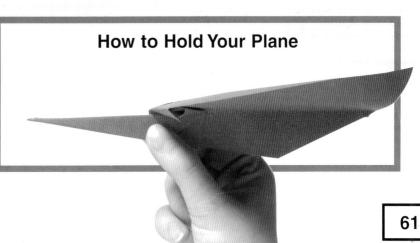

61

The Swift

By **Kunihiko Kasahara.**

Kasahara is one of the foremost origami designers in the world. Here he turns his skills to creating a highly acrobatic stunt plane, which swoops and turns just like a swift in flight.

2. Fold one end of the crease to meet the pinch mark.

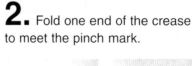

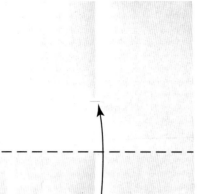

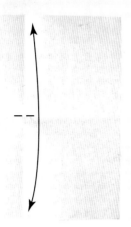

1. Start with a square, creased in half. Fold one end of the crease to the other, pinching lightly to find the center point.

3. Fold over both corners to meet the inside raw edge.

4. Fold each half of the nearest (folded) edge to lie along the vertical center crease. Leave a slight fudge factor.

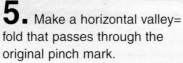

5. Make a horizontal valley=fold that passes through the original pinch mark.

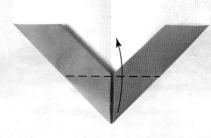

6. Fold the tip back outward. The exact distance isn't critical.

7. Carefully mountain-fold in half on the original central crease.

8. Make a crease that starts at the halfway point of the raw edge on the right and passes through the internal angle formed by the colored sections. Make sure that you have this clear in your mind before folding! Repeat with the other wing.

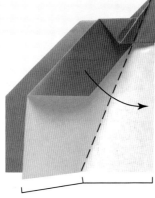

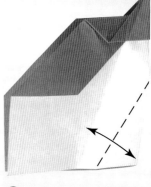

9. Precrease a valley=fold that will form the tail fin.

10. Push in the tail section using the creases shown. Reinforce the wing creases.

11. Make a valley crease between the two corners shown to shape the wings.

12. Complete.

FLIGHT ADVICE

Launch
As fast as possible, straight upward!

Trim
Alter the relative angle of the wings to the wingtips.

Creative Suggestions
Try folding the wingtips down instead of up.

How to Hold Your Plane

The Martin

By **Rikki Donachie.**

This is a very clever design, with a neat, flowing sequence. It ends up with two small flaps with which you can launch it.

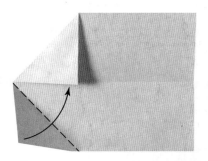

1. Start with a sheet of A-size paper creased in half. Fold two corners to the central crease at one end.

2. Take each folded edge to the inside raw edge, creasing as far as the center.

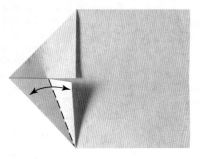

3. Take each folded edge to the center, creasing as far as the previous fold.

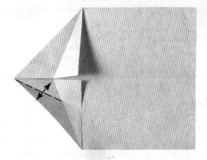

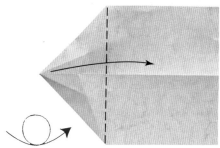

4. Turn the paper over and fold over the triangular section.

MAKING PAPER AIRPLANES

5. Use existing creases to flatten the paper into a point. Two small mountain creases are formed as you flatten the paper.

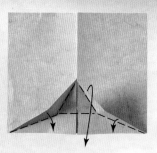

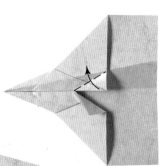

7. Fold the two outside corners to the center.

6. This is the result. Turn the paper over.

8. Fold the model in half from side to side.

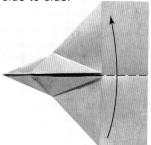

10. Fold out two small flaps, with which you can then launch the plane.

9. Fold over the wings, bisecting the angle of the nose.

11. Complete.

FLIGHT ADVICE

Launch
Open the body slightly and hold by the two fins. Adjust the wings to be at right angles to the body. Launch with medium strength.

Trim
Check that the wings are flat.

Creative Suggestions
Can you create a new plane starting at step 7?

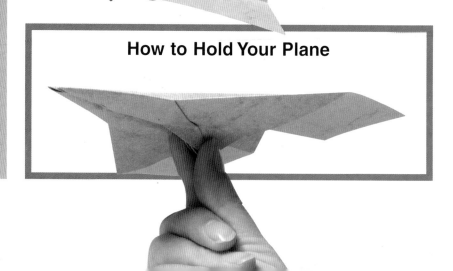

How to Hold Your Plane

Spinner

By **Nick Robinson.**

This design is more like a sycamore seed than a paper plane,
but just as much fun to fly!

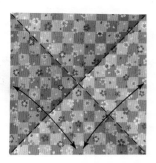

1. Start with a square, colored side facing upward. Fold in half from one corner to the opposite corner; repeat with the other two corners.

2. Turn the paper over and fold in half from side to opposite side. Repeat once more to form the "Union Jack" crease pattern.

3. Fold one corner into the center of the paper. The completed fold is shown on the other side.

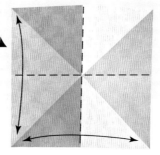

4. Collapse the paper using existing creases only.

MAKING PAPER AIRPLANES

5. This is the result. Fold an outside corner into the center of the paper. Repeat on the matching corner and the two corners underneath.

6. Narrow the flaps by folding to the center, once again repeating the fold on the three matching flaps.

7. This is the result. Fold one layer upward, turn the paper over, and repeat on the matching flap.

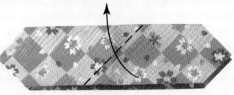

8. You should now have flat sections of paper top and bottom. Fold over one of the loose flaps at an angle of 45 degrees.

9. This is the result. Repeat underneath.

10. Complete!

FLIGHT ADVICE

Launch
Hold the model as high as possible and release.

Trim
Adjust the angles of the "wing" flaps.

Creative Suggestions
Try making the flaps wider or more narrow.

How to Hold Your Spinner

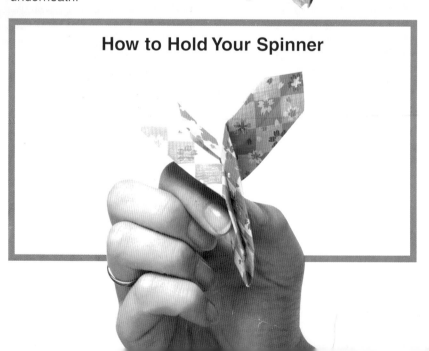

Art-deco Wing

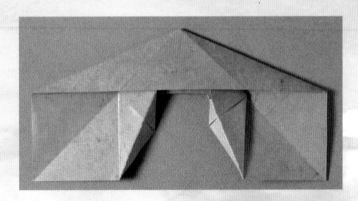

By *Michael LaFosse.*

This is a flying-wing design, something that is quite hard to achieve using paper. LaFosse is a highly gifted creator, and has produced many stunning origami pieces, as well as many unusual and interesting flying designs.

1. Start with a square of paper. Fold from corner to corner.

2. Fold both ends of the folded edge to the top corner.

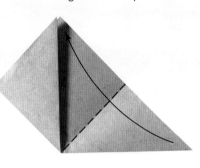

3. Take the left-hand vertical edge to the outside edge, crease, and unfold.

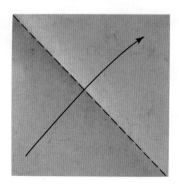

4. Lift and squash, using the crease that you have just made.

5. Repeat on the other side.

6. Turn the paper over and fold over the large triangular flap.

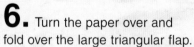

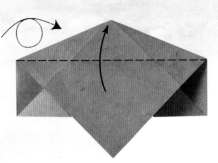

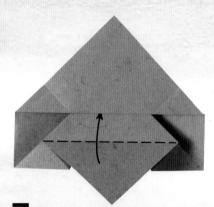

7. Fold the smaller triangular flap upward, tucking it into the pocket.

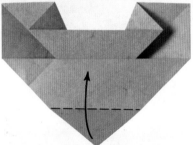

8. Rotate the paper to the position shown. Fold the triangular flap in half.

9. Fold the same section in half once again.

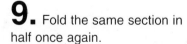

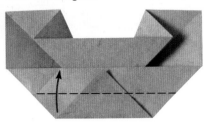

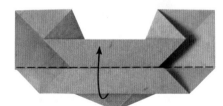

10. Swing the flap over again.

11. Rotate the paper. Fold the two small outside corners to lie along the horizontal edge.

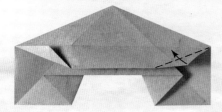

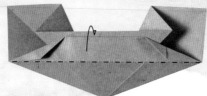

12. Rotate the paper once more. Tuck the flap inside the pocket.

13. Again, rotate the paper. Getting dizzy? Lift the central flap and fold it upward. At the same time, fold the paper on either side inward, allowing it to flatten neatly. Check the next picture if you need help.

14. This is the result. Tuck the paper into the pocket underneath.

15. Finally, add two small mountain folds to form fins.

FLIGHT ADVICE

Launch
Hold the plane in the center, from behind. Launch with a gentle forward push.

Trim
Adjust the two fins.

Creative Suggestions
Create your own flying wing using step 6 as a starting point.

How to Hold Your Plane

Rocket

By **Nick Robinson.**
Identical in shape to an existing nonflying design, this fold
actually flies. You can also have fun placing a box in the yard,
then trying to drop the rocket into it from
as far away as possible.

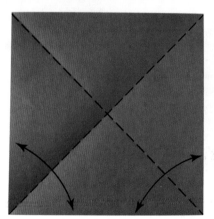

2. Turn the paper over and
fold in half from side to
side both ways.

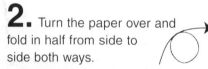

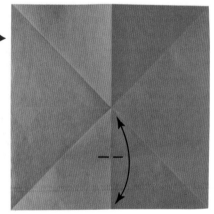

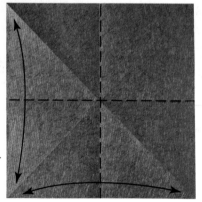

1. Start with a large
square of paper. Now
crease both diagonals.

3. Turn the paper back over
and add a small crease marking
the halfway point.

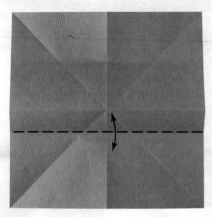

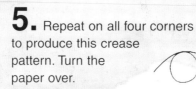

5. Repeat on all four corners to produce this crease pattern. Turn the paper over.

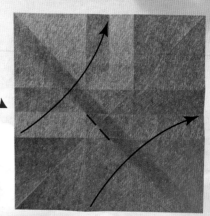

4. Fold the central crease to touch the mark made in the last step. Crease right across the paper.

6. Fold a corner over so that the location points shown meet up. Check the next picture for guidance.

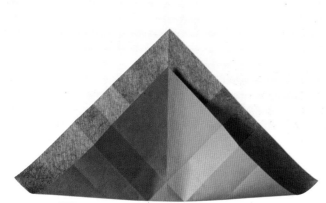

7. Make a small crease between the points shown. Then turn the paper back over.

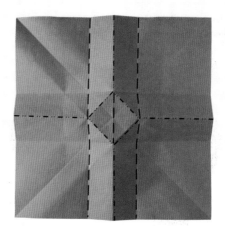

8. All of these creases are in the paper, but you will need to alter some as shown. Twist the center of the paper counterclockwise as it collapses into the position shown in the next diagram.

9. Here is the move in progress. Make sure that you are only folding the creases shown and are not adding any new ones!

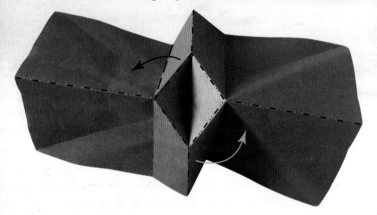

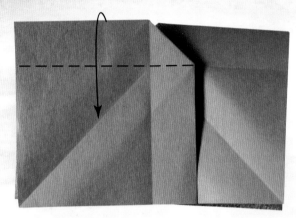

10. Well done. Fold the loose layer at the top left downward.

11. Swing the hidden layer up from beneath so that the paper is symmetrical.

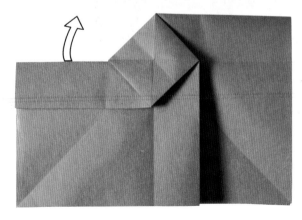

12. Crease the halfway point of the lower triangular section. Repeat on the three other sides.

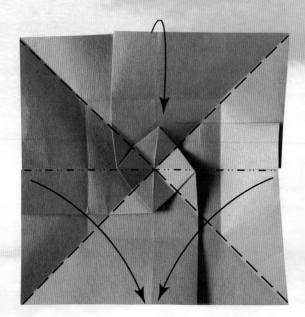

13. Imagine that the paper is a plain square and collapse it into the water-bomb base.

14. Take one of the folded edges to the vertical center edge, crease firmly, and unfold.

15. Swing the corner up and to the right, starting at the center of the lower edge. The crease passes through a meeting point of two creases (shown in gray). See the next picture for guidance.

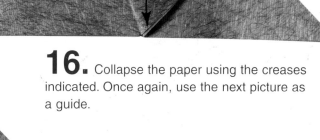

16. Collapse the paper using the creases indicated. Once again, use the next picture as a guide.

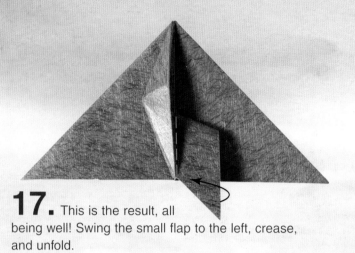

17. This is the result, all being well! Swing the small flap to the left, crease, and unfold.

18. Repeat the last four steps on the three remaining flaps, then arrange the layers into a cross, with each flap at 45 degrees to the next. Complete!

How to Hold Your Plane

FLIGHT ADVICE

Launch
This design should be thrown as hard as possible at an angle of about 45 degrees. A higher angle will produce a shorter distance.

The Twin

By **Nick Robinson.**

This shows how, with a bit of imagination, exciting new designs can be developed from existing ones. This one uses the landscape (page 52) and canard (page 30) designs, and with minor adaptations, joins them into a flying model that you couldn't achieve using a single sheet.

Start with the landscape design folded up to step 7, then unfolded completely, and the canard folded to completion, then unfolded to step 5.

1. Make a horizontal crease that joins the main crease intersections on either side.

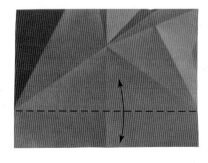

2. Fold over the lower corners so that their inside edges meet the two existing creases.

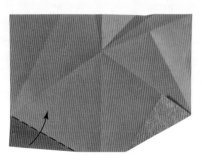

3. Swing over the lower section on the crease made in step 1.

4. Take the canard and fold the tip of the upper square in half toward you. Then mountain-fold the rest of it behind on an existing (valley) crease.

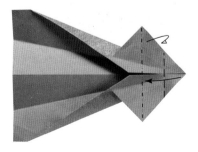

MAKING PAPER AIRPLANES

5. Slide the same flap behind the layer of the landscape section and start to reform the wing creases of the landscape.

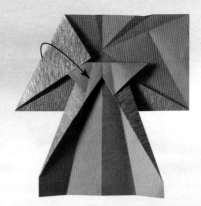

6. Reform another fold.

7. Reform the right-hand section, tucking the paper within, as in the original design.

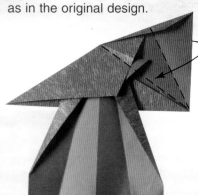

8. Reform the main body creases of the canard, extending the creases through the extra paper of the landscape.

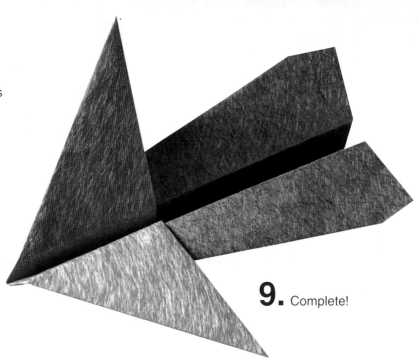

9. Complete!

How to Hold Your Plane

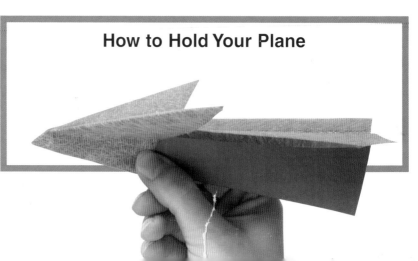

Index

Credits

Thanks to: Sarah and David King and Colin Bowling.

To Michael LaFosse, Rikki Donachie, Kunihiko Kasahara, and Robin Glynn for allowing their designs to be published. Alison, Daisy, Nick, Gomez, Matilda, Big Dave, and Bob, all part of my extended family. John, Mick, and Joe for helping keep my fingers flexible.

To paper-folders everywhere for their fellowship, inspiration, and willingness to share ideas; and to Ken Blackburn for pushing paper-airplane records to the limit and beyond!

The Author: *Nick Robinson*
An I.T. lecturer, web author, and writer, Nick lives in Sheffield, England. He has been folding for over twenty years and is a council member of the British Origami Society. He also maintains its website and edits its magazine. He has appeared on television in the U.K. and abroad and has created numerous designs for magazines, television, and other media. Over one-hundred-and-fifty of his original origami creations have been published in fifteen countries around the world. His website is www.12testing.net. As a former professional musician, he still performs live, solo, improvised, ambient guitar concerts.

Origami Contacts
If you enjoyed folding the projects in this book, you really should contact your nearest origami society. It can supply you with paper, new designs, a newsletter, and, most importantly, many new friends!

Origami U.S.A.: www.origami-usa.org

British Origami Society: www.britishorigami.org.uk